It Rains Diamonds on Saturn

Selected Poems – 1984 to 2020

Jéanpaul Ferro

"There is always some madness in love. But there is also always some reason in madness."

—Friedrich Nietzsche

"The cemeteries of the world are full of indispensable men."

—Charles de Gaulle

Credits

Letters from America |
Black Magnolias Literary Journal
Digital Americana Magazine
13 Magazine

The River That Runs Away From Paradise |
Pedestal Magazine
Corium Magazine
Jellyfish Whispers

The Risk of Absurdity |
Dublin Quarterly
Istanbul Review
Pacific Review
Pedestal Magazine
Kudzu Review

Dreams of Men |
Dark Sky Magazine
Asia Literary Review

Black Man Speaking Below Federal Hill |
The Hawaii Review

India, 1937 |
Bathtub Gin Literary Journal

Ravensbrück Clothes |
Ragazine
Cider House Press

You Know Too Much About Flying Saucers * |
Fieldstone Review
Steel Toe Review
* Nominated for the 2012 Pushcart Prize

The Secret State of Everything * |
Willows Wept Review
  * Nominated for the Pushcart Prize

Drop the Veil Center Stage |
Toronto Quarterly Review

You Are Only What You Can Carry |
13 Magazine

The Underworld |
The Medulla Review

The Book of Twilights |
Decades Review
Steel Toe Review
Avalon Literary Review

The Last Time We Ever Went to Charlestown Beach |
Barrelhouse Magazine

Living a Life at Night |
Columbia Review
Loch Raven Review

Arrete! C'est ici L'Empire de la Mort— |
Emerson Review
Salzburg Review
Toronto Quarterly

Mohegan Bluffs |
The Providence Journal

Late Summer In Rhode Island |
National Public Radio
NPR "This I Believe" series

Cuba * |
The Arava Review
* Nominated for the Pushcart Prize
Gentle Strength Quarterly
Litchfield Literary Review

This Much |
Pedestal Magazine

No. 5, 1948 |
Contemporary American Voices

Gun, With Occasional Music |
The Providence Journal
Contemporary American Voices
Upstreet Magazine

John Updike |
Contemporary American Voices
Istanbul Literary Review

Into the City |
Pedestal Magazine

Armageddon Days |
The Rose & Thorn Literary Review

Letter from a Soldier |
Sierra Nevada Review
Big Bridge Anthology
Gander Press Review
Cider House Press

The Dream House |
Chaffey Review
Gander Press Review

Becoming X |
Letter From A Soldier |
Gun, With Occasional Music |
In Our Own Words: A Generation Defining Itself Anthology

Life on Mars |
The Medulla Review
Loch Raven Review

Becoming X |
l'allure des mots

79 Degree Probability of Loss |
The Newport Review
Magnolia: A Florida Journal of Literary and Fine Arts
Napalm and Novocain Review
Pedestal Magazine

Gun, With Occasional Music |
Letter From a Soldier |
Song Sheets |
Parlor Lit Magazine
Underground Magazine

Color-Fields |
The Rose & Thorn Literary Review

Young Brother |
Arts &Understanding Magazine
Black Lawrence Press 2011: Art & Understanding: The Anthology

The Abortion |
The Rose & Thorn Literary Review;
The Taj Mahal Review; The Hunted News

Red Diamonds |
Review Americana
Digital Americana Magazine
Istanbul Review

The Book of Mary |
Contemporary American Voices
Wilderness House Literary Review
Istanbul Literary Review

The Hours Happened |
The Externalist

Throw Like a Girl |
JMWW Quarterly Journal
Emerson Review
Digital Americana Magazine

The Waves |
Bryant Literary Review

Young Frankenstein |
Connecticut Review

Contents

Letters from America

We always thought you should be proud
of your black skin, but you never were—

Black is the *Shakespeare* of all color.

It is carnal like white is carnal, like ocean blue,
like an African red rain in the dead of night;

this unquenchable essence; something cupped
in the brand fires of the plains; half the day being
black, the nighttime sky full of an all encompassing
blackness that travels on and on out into the universe.

And look at you!

Your eyes are the same hue as dusk over New Orleans.
Your hair like curling wisps of cloud reflecting atop the Nile.
Your black feet always tapping to a perfect juxtaposition
of Mississippi Jazz; a rat-tat-tat.

Black is the rough-hewn clay of all hues of vibrant color,
it is the color of rebellion, of justice,
it is the color of the soul of James Brown,
Johnny Cash, Muhammad Ali, Hank Aaron, the
Beatles, Africa, and India, and even in deep rooted
strands of DNA no one else can see.

On the moon the earth sits in a wet pool of black space,
a blue jewel-spot set in the dark tone of the solar system;

look around you at all that is magnificent;
black everywhere!

It is obvious that God's favorite color is undoubtably black—
it is what one sees when they close their eyes to dream.

The Risk of Absurdity

Tattooed and pierced,
come dance atop the waterfires,
orange glow of the sparkling comics,
all shambled and wild-haired,
mad scientists, mad poets,
all the un-interesting things of the seven other elements,
an uncommon girl, her mouth tender like cinnamon,
go currents, shoulder to shoulder,
the truth no religion at all,
life with all its untraceable tracks,
God everywhere you look,
incredibly mad to live! frantic as hell to live!
you must race to it all to even live,
make those bombs fade away,
telephone wire to telephone wire,
anamorphic dream, sending birds askew
with microchips to fly from Mexico
to Maine,
two blushing suns in the simmering blue waves,
in the waves of anxious music,
footsteps atop rigorous black hands,
the CIA, the Creation of Adam,
fuming in iron, magnesia, and sulfur,
in the allies, panic-stricken at times:
in dreams, in stars; life just like that,
offering nothing but confusion,
but you must embrace it; look for it in others;
see the curve of the earth in rear view mirrors,
atop the cotton-candy fog of the autumn valleys,

up there it lives in the wood smoke of the old-world chimneys,
in the books under the blue starry library roofs,
you're not alive without this sensation of death in it,
with every aching sinew, aching of loss,
desirous of everything that is commonplace
to man, being in love when it is as effortless
as dying and waking, in the haunting loneliness
of evening, where you will do it all your life,
where in this suffering twilight you will realize
that you are crazy enough to think you can change
things, change things in this great, wobbling, stabbing
dream we all call our tumultuous world.

The Abortion

When I came home I could not find you,

Only the milk-fed veal pounded out on
the counter and red tomatoes and basil
and rosemary cooking on the stove.

The Book of Mary (America)

I can't remember waking up in love with you,
because I don't remember falling asleep in love with you.

You and I are a million words that don't exist yet,
startled one hour, starving for each other the next,
both of us underdeveloped in our togetherness,
cutting each other's wrists in the kitchen sink,
blood the color Henry Miller would write it,
in a moment when we both realize *there is no use lingering*,
pain like God's pain, his eyes bulging from the wars,
through the blue room you can feel it in your throat,
you tear your clothes off, hang yourself by your hands with rope,
you are the most secret thing in the world, rain on a dark child's face,
you break me because you want all of me,
you love me because the pain is that enormous,
this is right now, tonight, yesterday, a million years in the future,
I drive in a yellow cab looking for you everywhere,
"Come," I hear you saying; "Come," I hear in darkness;
"People are just things," you keep signing to me in my hand—
as though we can both just edit a lifetime full of mistakes.

79 Degree Probability of Loss

What beautiful death there is in Madonna de Campiglio,
the peasant people frozen in ice in dance,
the slopes of Austria, and now they call it Italy,
another place you must come, one more dream to put your trust in,

and you can't believe you'll ever do it again,
swimming in the light and shadows where you've drowned,
the gum arabic and green volatilize of valle Verzasca—
the river where you saw the diver from Lucerne go down three
times,
the way you held his girlfriend, the river from the glacier,
minion and nonpareil, crystalline, his body preserved,
Russian experiment in the stone houses of Sonogno,

the ache in my body as you ease yourself against me,
the way your legs cower out, the ecstasy in your pain,
in the white under your flesh in your bones,
the risk, the knife of your spine,
and I take it, twist and turn and bludgeon it,
and the body moves, consumes all of me, and you give in,
and you die in a way too, so cold here in the Dolomites,
always writing by candlelight, the bathroom out in the hallway,
and dance without music—

the sound of your hands against the piano back in the States.

Dreams of Men

The sky in North Korea always leads to China,
dark during the day, bright plutonium yellow at night,

dogs sell human body parts along the country roads here,
humans cut off other human's legs in the camps simply out
of revenge,

there is neither a half full nor a half empty glass,
there is neither a half full nor a half empty soul,

everyone knows the day they are going to die in North Korea,

there is torture and a life sentence in the political prisons
for when you are caught (it does not matter for what),

you have a 5-foot-by-5-foot underground cell,
you are hit, you are raped, you are tortured,
you creep, you crawl, and you cower,
you are crashed, you are experimented on,
you are rushed off your feet by freezing water,
you are poisoned, starved, gassed, you are cut up,

you are told your dead children's names over and over;

I smashed my fingertips so they would kill me,
but they laughed at me for over 3 ½ years instead,

I huddled in the corner all night long to try and dream—

dream of my fingertips touching the wet sands of an ocean again,
dream of the bright garden stars rising out in our backyard,
dream of your hips with cinnamon and parsley,
dream of your body raising sunward like a blue sunflower,

dream of flying south over the distant mountain tops,
so we could die together in a beautiful peace.
Black Man Speaking Below Federal Hill

On my black face all blackness shines,
rivers and temples and dreams too:
a murmur of life that still survives amid
the tall Egyptian grasses,
a ghost of what we once were all along the
banks of the blue Egyptian Nile.

But you want to put me to death like you always do,
silence my voice that haunts you from the pain and horror
of the past, the present, and the future still;

but all of life is nothing but horror and pain—a warm crest
of an ocean wave right as it climaxes on over you.

Throw Like a Girl

We thought there was blood on our hands
from all the strawberries that we had picked.

When I looked up the late summer sun was setting
directly behind her head, darkening her brown hair
like it was iron bars on a cage.

She wore a white dress, the one with maroon polka dots,
her delicate hands holding a bucket of strawberries, a
beautiful smile caught in the exuberance of her eyes.

But off in the distance I could hear a stillness from
the wind dying down.

"It's the end of summer," she said, standing there
in the field like a ghost.

Looking down at the folds in her hands, she said:
"I think I'm broken in six-hundred and thirty-seven
different places."

Red, Red Moon

I awoke in the canyon under a red, red moon.
Next to me I heard an Arab brother crying out:
"You know? You know? You know?"
And I said: *"I know! I know! I know!"*

I awoke atop Mt. Everest in the midst of a white cloud.
Within the snowstorm I heard an Indian spirit praying:
"You know? You know? You know?"
And I said: *"I know! I know! I know!"*

I awoke in the ghetto in a graffiti filled room.
Outside in the hallway I heard a loud bang, and then
someone shout: *"You know? You know? You know?"*
And I said: *"I know! I know! I know!"*

I awoke in the desert under the shade of a date palm.
Jesus came signing to me in my hand, and he was saying:
"You know? You know? You know?"
And I said: *"I know! I know! I know!"*

I awoke in the sea under a heap of green, green waves after
the bomb fell from a drone. I was about to let go when I
heard your ghost scream out to me: *"You know? You know?
You know?"*
And I whispered softly: *"I know. I know. I know."*

The Last Day We Ever Went to Charlestown Beach

On the last day we ever went to Charlestown Beach,
a million dragonflies came floating by in the air,
green little explosions in jewels seemingly everywhere
from out of nowhere,

A girl sitting there in an orange bikini said to you:
"This is the last day you'll ever be alive!"

We both laughed; and we drank to both yesterday and tomorrow.
And then you said to me with great fervor: *You'll never forget
this day! You'll never forget this day! You'll never forget this day!"*

Song Sheets

She says she wants someone perfect,
reliable, and at least with a steady job,
someone as beautiful as the fresco of Moldavia
that she has up on her bedroom wall up behind her bed,
its rich, deep landscape full of the misery of the Assyrians
and the Persians,
golds and reds and a beautiful calcium copper still intact,
human figures converting to Islam in a shimmering mosaic of
tesserae and Egyptian blue.

It would be a better world if we could all simply be who
we need to be; I don't know why she is always trying
to change me.

"Christ didn't die on a cross," she tells me in a fit
of anger.

"Nothing's perfect," I say.

The Underworld

In the sacred grove between Tralleis and Nysa,
the one between 13th Street and Eye Street,
where the snow-covered grass in the park bubbles
over red like borscht atop the seven radioactive minds;

seven dreams of the oracles, each one attached to the
great American work of betrayal: the beauty of napalm
in the 6-degree winter air; the Isolationists, the
Interventionists, the Whigs, the Libertarians,
the Raza Unida, the World Socialists, the blue state
verses the red state pols; all meeting with their Fellow Crafts
down at The Palms for blood steaks and shots; the greatest
generation selling out their souls for a C-Note, lust and greed
stuffed into bank bags of willful short-sightedness,
the industrial and military machine opening union
shop down at the corner of Henry Hudson and Main,
getting truth and justice all junked up on methamphetamine,
the ivory buff and golden marble so worn off nobody can
even recognize it straight anymore, right being left, left now
blind, no one getting out of the cave to see the light of day;

planes shuddering into buildings now, bombs going off
in the London lobby of the hotel; the old boss, same as
the new boss down at Royal Albert Hall; the blue phenomenon
of the Perito Moreno melting; Mississippi rain everlasting;
the Outer Banks you used to know as a kid now ten miles
out from where Kill Devil Hills used to be;

oil pumping hard from its veins, the sky full of this boisterous
noise, everyone pointing fingers everywhere else; some
holding a Bible, a Torah, and the Qur'an in their blood
soaked hands; pimps, pushers, bold-faced liars, lobbyists,
Black Ops, the Ninth Circuit Court of Appeals for ten-time
liars and cheats, fame whores, demagogues, plutocratic idiots,
all the filthy vermin of this good earth as God watches intently
from the Memphis terrace of his hotel room, both his hands
clinched down hard like fists from all the wars he sees;

and on Christmas morning, the Pope is getting breakfast
down at Denny's, twenty minutes before he must bless the
latest war of Donald Trump and his imprudent masses.

Veronica Lake

In the picture we stood along the bow
of the glass-bottom boat,
your blonde hair brushed halfway
across one side of your face like you were
trying to be Veronica Lake that day,

turquoise-blue water surrounding us on four sides,

sweeping black sheets of rain

     f f f f f f
       a a a a a a
        l l l l l l
         l l l l l l
          i i i i i
   n n n n n
    g g g g g
      in the
        distance,

both our souls slowly fading to gray,

the only sound the tired way we always
seem to bring anguish and hurt upon ourselves;
and martini glasses!

a gentle twinkle of crystal as it clanked in a toast
to the last pink light of the day (quietly slipping away).

The River That Runs Away From Paradise

In the green afterlife of twilight,
only seconds after you left the bar of drunken soldiers,
twelve hours after you buried your greatest loss,
buried it within the jungle, set it ablaze in leftover scraps
of funeral pyre,

the sky shuts you off from the sun, entrenches you in a darkness
that is right, the leopards watching you from their branches,

escape; where is this? death enters; it brings comfort only from the
furthest place from home, East of Eden, that desolate place of
nowhere, that place where men and woman have no names.

You dream big now, dream like you should have dreamt all along,
in the steps of Marco Polo, down to a hero's journey, to a place you
have never seen before—*Caño Cristales*, the most beautiful river
in the world, the river of five colors, a place you can be no one and
nowhere at once, a place that is only recorded in the secret Atlas
of the World, the one every Mason hides on their person.

Five days later … you are lost somewhere inside of Columbia,
traveling down a dirt and pot-hole filled road, a road going through
parts of Serrania de la Macarena that only the guerrilla forces
have traveled before.

The Earth stands still; you see a billboard ominously posted along
the way:

The war is over. … There is another life now.

Noon comes under pale blue skies; soon you can hear the river, its cries softly out to you, like a child wailing lost far from home, you begin to sob because it is this dream you have been drinking just to get you along.

Your steps are slow now as you approach the river from its sand banks, sweat dripping off of you.

A riverbed stretches out in front of you into sempiternity; yes, it is finally right there for you:

cascades traveling atop the autumn foliage of another planet, twenty-seven different shades of the green of Columbia shifting back and forth—*verde, esmeralda, aceituna, savia, arma*; stark magenta waterfalls, intense craters of blood-red and notoriety, cells of rainbow floating downriver into the arched shade of the trees, yellow sand as it sparkles under the late afternoon sun.

You stand there in disbelief. And you believe in God for that moment. And for another lonely moment caught in experiment, a moment you wished would have never come, you actually dream that it was the moment before.

Red Diamonds

You are beautifully concise,
like a rower on the Charles,
liquid when I try to hold you,
accidental music when I try to leave,

all through the New England evenings
fire shivers orange/gold amid the campsites
down below the mountains,

we make up stories to keep each other
amused, men who turn into elephant cinders,
women who fight like moonlight in the sky,

"Don't kiss her," you always write
in your suicide notes.

"Don't marry him," I always scribble over
your wedding invitations.

No wonder no one else wants me,
no wonder everyone wants to know me,
someone tells me you are the art of fiction,
I think you are the sound of wind in the palms,
a million little prayers to God from all his misled children,

I want to share you, but only a little,
a naked piece here, a naked piece there, naked on the rooftops,
I want all the good Brazilian pieces for myself,
the ancient, smooth parts like the inside of cake,

some parts that are as old as Jerusalem,
some parts that are pierced and narrow and need a vow,
maybe I will take all of you, you'd like that,
you'd like turquoise waves over your bronze body, too,
you'd like it if we rode turtles across the Indian Ocean,
you'd like it if I wrote poems, like this one,
with your curved and brown body turning on every word.

The Nine Billion Names For One God

If a man understands a poem,
he shall have troubles.

—Mark Strand

She enters my head like ten quarter stars, all through
my corporal body, downward, a liquid warm, soothing,
wet like ancient amber, all these sinuous roots bursting
forth from my heart, spinning 'round, a glowing Ferris
wheel at night on Coney Island, joyful as pink fireworks,
shooting up like coastal redwoods, Hyperion, Helios, and
Icarus.

India, 1937

By late afternoon we had killed all the tigers,
lined them up, one by one, in the grassy field,
stood with one leg up on their orange/white bodies,
smiled toward the camera for the picture they would
be sending back home for (prosperity's sake).

You Are Only What You Can Carry

She jumped from the great heights of Alumni Stadium,
all her shirts in her closet tied together by the arms,
her last words to me so beautifully wrought like springtime
sparrows flying upside down together in trapeze,
forming the shape of a woman until her mind had shattered,

all these black and wrecked pieces of glass falling helplessly
to the ground.

Desire Brings Me Back

My God of mercy split into the faces of ten-thousand strangers:

Ih a/at Y (r,t) = - h2/2m Ñ² Y (r,t) V (r,t) Y (r,t,)

the wave function, defined over space and time;

young brunette suicide bomber exploded for all the world to see,

delight, anger, confusion; someone else's daughter, sister, aunt, cousin, friend;

posted online for prosperity for everyone else to see,

all the currencies of our modern and anonymous Internet life:

the non-random choice of our own narcissism.

Ravensbrück Clothes

Within the Greek Revival columns
of the Providence Athenaeum,
under the brick reds of the Rare Book room,
I began to hallucinate in front of the books
of wars and wars and wars;

I dream backwards to German soldiers
picking through all these brand new Ravensbrück
clothes, like ghosts perched up without bodies,
shirt, skirt, dress, these ghostly empty coats floating
through blue air,

picking up watches from piles of watches,
combing through wedding rings in pile after pile
of wedding rings,

over there a pile of bracelets,

things belonging to the Jewish blond girls
of Magdeburg, Koblenz, Hamburg;

sometimes you can still hear all those soldiers
echoes:

oh, it feels better to take the things of the most
pretty ones, feels best to kill them the slowest—

young, fresh-faced, faces minted anew like
bags of bank coins, this kind of beautiful face
that stares out into forever,

the watchmen slowly letting them burn
into this warmth for their hands, their young
cosmic bodies floating up right out into the furnace
of the wintry sun.

The Book of Twilights

We sat below the neon-lit palms like we always did when
you were small, a rose and gold colored sky between us and
the lightening crackling down a hundred miles away,
columns and hives of black cloud rising, rising upward like
gods atop the horizon of strange ocean off in the distance,

I remember your young and frightened eyes looking up at me
for comfort before you started to outgrow me—

    that brittle sound of the clamshell road beneath our feet
    under the moonlight as we made our way home.

Becoming X

I could no longer grow in the ground
with any impact like everyone else,

the brown shards of me spread out along
the gold hued bottom of the Washita River,

all my signifiers indistinguishable in this
new world of modern gadgetry,

because we all want lives as soft and comfy
as a pop song,

relationships like that first second when you
meet someone:

so subversively surreal, it always feels like crawling
along the ground up to the sacred altars.

But I could not escape my own personal hell,
broadcasting myself so I would trip through my
brain all night long *forever*,

my perfect soul spinning 'round and 'round
up in the ether,

my AR-15 going off all over the campus—
until I become somebody really important
and every cable channel put me on the news.

Letter From A Soldier

I look for you in the dark,
far beyond the Massachusetts woods
near the New Hampshire border,
where the gray wolves hide at the
edge line of the chestnut trees;

all night long as the rockets
rain down inside my head just
a little bit harder.

I go through all the imaginary alleys
as the buildings start to come down
and everything begins to turn to ash.

But I am just a little bit broken,
broke in all the right places—

a million little jewels that split apart

    all across the ground.

Young Frankenstein

We sat under the blinking neon bible
in Times Square—you and I in the year
that got away:

You bought me some white carnations;
I tried to buy us some more time on eBay;

you always liked to use metaphors on the
last Friday of every year,

door latch/brass socket,
contras wrapped in red poppies;

She wrote on a napkin: Oh, please don't
send me coconuts through the mail again;

but that is what you *do* when you're out in
Hawaii, I said;

The next day I flew across the lower 48,
because two can play this game,

After landing, I went and sat out on the big island
waiting for her, but she never came;

So, this is it? I'll have the small cottage down
along the volcanic beach all to myself?

I'll listen to the German tourists tell me all the
things their prejudice already knows about America;

How immense this on-again/off-again life of ours
has become;

we measure each other by the distance alone,
the coconuts piling up out front;

until anonymous sends me the paper that lays out
exactly what happened to you while I wasn't paying
attention.

This Much

I watched her walk out the blue door,

so at night I took her by the feet out into
the ten kinds of darkness,

her mouth whispering the way the Internet
whispers poetry,

forks and spoons packed up like we're
on the go again,

drunk in night sweats in the time machine
on our way to equilibrium,

please! I scream; *I can't do this anymore!*
she screams;

until finally we both let go, hay in both
of our hair, our minds/souls undone,

because twenty years in the future I hear
the pain I put in her voice right now,

so I bring her back home and place her in
bed with the cool covers tucked in beneath
her chin,

her mind never knowing the before and after
of everything I had to undo (just for her).

Cuba

We hid amid the swaying fields of sugar cane
when Castro overthrew that fool, Fulgencio,

you in your libidinous red dress that kept
all the men of Plaza Vieja very happy, every day
a procession after the bullfights and the executions;

I think I was dead every morning I was without you,
the statues of the city cold, but I understood them,

at night we drank and danced and then we retired to watch
all the old cars going fast under the trestles,

In the daytime, I worked right near San Cristobal,
trying to write like Hemingway on our old typewriter,

but you cured me for my lack of a reputation,
me, arriving home to find you naked and wet in bed,
leaving me hungry for your soul like a wallet longing
for crisp green bills;

but then change and revolution came!

and we were all happy and afraid as we hid in the fields,
dreaming of the former, hoping for tomorrow,
hiding for a day that turned into the last fifty years;

And now I am old, and you have already gone,
nothing to quench my thirst like things used to do,

Jesus! I'm tired of waiting for Cuba to change!

Cuba is both a truth and a fiction, a great story of lust
and of craving,

A country that longs for tomorrow to be like yesterday,
and for yesterday to be like tomorrow. *Amen.*

The Waves

In the afternoon, when the sky
is almost out of sun,

when you would normally cling to her,
let her run all the way down,

any other day when it is simply a play,
an hour, a second in which you can say
anything,

let it sing, let it ascend, let it plummet down
like it is rain—

into the shadows, into the moon-blanched seconds
as she says *goodbye*;

deftly, as all the traffic signals are turning red;
and you know no one is waiting for you
when you get home;

downtown, maybe at 10:30 when you can still
hear her words, where you can remember:

the convergence of her body beneath you,
the confused and spiraling waterfall going
upwards, the wildflowers blossoming all
around her bed,

you see it in people as they go in and out of doors,
in their steps as they go up and down from city hall,

a homeless man next to a rich man next to the man that
you used to be—

you look up at the city lights; you can see the dark
imperfection floating atop the three rivers,

a car honks to let you go, but it is ten years ago
and you just can't hear it,

people's voices fill the air, everyone laughing
as they skate around in darkness in Kennedy Plaza,

wisps of bodies in the naked streetlight
falling down into this useless beauty,

and you can say anything, you think, you can say all
the things that you are in love with,

stomp on them, save them in the bank, hold onto them
forever, or let them go—

down the river, or all the way down to the ocean
into the burnt blue of its rolling waves.

The Dream House

0.0: The dream house

Her soul was the color of God,
a thunderhead of apple red, and in wavelengths,
vestigial hips and thighs/the drunkenness
that comes thereafter;

the palpable lure of Everest, the way you
conquer it when it is easily conquering you,
translucent as night, a shrouded thing to wrap
and unwrap;

midnight in a blind dress, the sticky and
beautiful idea on the tips of our tongues,
India and Pakistan, fingers in her bible,
a last visage of 1960's hope;

two contradictory quarks, but it all makes sense,
an autobiography of *tomorrow* written in *today*,

two empty hotels along the Hudson River,
two bridges drenched in sky—flailing, clawing,

a mirror of the sun for a thousand years.

The Secret State of Everything

We came by moonlight to Cuba,
washed up on her shores with the giant catfish,
drunk and fragrant like melon rinds,

wedged between each other and the sands,
your long hair, wet, adorned in the color of delicate lemons,
your kiss a topaz held against the morning light,

pinned against each other like we are cuffed together,
our every move sticky and blistering in the heat,
two prisoners, caught on an island we cannot escape,

swim, you think;

go on and on forever, I think;

we scream, but no one hears our pleas,

you squeeze my hand, and we swallow everything together,
merging, wrangling back against the waves (to hide)
from the rest of humanity.

Armageddon Days

In a phone booth at the corner of 47th and 9th
outside Amy's Bread, all of New York City
steeped in bottle-green and neo red,
too weak to seek out what's appropriate tonight,
both my legs waterfalls in her living memory,
the *New York Times* squawking about another war
in the Middle East we need to wet our beaks.

Jesus, pick the phone, need to talk A.S.A.P.

I see it in the look on every worn-out face,
eyes secretly dreaming in poetry instead of death,
living a life they've got—right or wrong, imperfect or not;
just going on, sometimes through a raving madness,
sometimes through a pitch dark no one else can even relate to—
I've actually never heard so much brilliant singing as when
I've been in such a dark space, air whooshing by,
cars splashing water.

Jesus, you there? maybe you can come—*quick!*

There is something to say for not saying anything
at all; right or wrong; solitary or strong; peace or in-fighting.

I'll be who I am; you can be whoever you want;
all the wind in our veins growing colder by the minute,
nothing wrong or downtrodden or broken changing
mutating into something better, into light, or color;

a million faces to see when you only need to see one:

hello? anyone there? hello? hello? hello?

Poem #27

I read poetry by poets who have never met ten
Puerto Rican girls singing and dying at a funeral;

never saw an old man about to slit the throat of one
of his own fine goats.

Have you ever seen a man take the life of his own wife
with a club?

Have you ever seen one wave take the life of ten thousand
men, women, and children like they were simply dust?

I have seen things that a slip of paper cannot hold.

I have kissed the brunette hair of the woman that I was
in love with while she was lying there in her casket.

I have written a song for my son who died at age three.

I have remembered long goodbyes like they were ten
thousand winters in Soviet Russia.

I have seen tanks run over a man until he was down to
nothing.

I have seen a field piled high with the pale limbs of men
and women who were stacked up like cord wood like they
did not even matter.

I have seen things in the nature of man that I wish I could
erase from my eyes, so this page could be blank—

but it isn't.

Life on Mars

In a cone of yellow light the spaceship came over me,
up I was lifted into their city of true believers,

colorless cities of light, spherical with the same oneness
only found in nature, all of our past heroes already there:

        Anaïs Nin,
                Aristotle,
Picasso,
                    H.P. Lovecraft,
      Kurt Cobain;

and they had redwoods and tall waterfalls and orange
hued canyons, deep blue oceans full of whales and mile
long squid,

and in their deep green sky existed all their Gods all of the time,
and I was naked and perfect and unafraid at every turn and
moment,

and over the airwaves they had me repeat my lines,
broadcast it out into their perfect minds that could hear
every thought all of the time.

And at night in my new home I lie there awake, staring up
into their bright green sky,

not thinking about God who was right there, but dreaming
about *you* instead, your naked body clutched tightly up against
my soul that was trembling,

the scent of wood smoke on us like when we were wet and out
camping,

dreams of our dog and the ice storm when the electricity went out,
how everything was frozen like platinum;

and you quoted Anaïs Nin right before the power came back on:
We don't see things as they are, we see things as we are, you
whispered;

and right then the telephone rang as the lights came on up; and it was
your father calling, frantic, to tell you that your mother had died.

After Leaving Ms. Mackenzie

I retraced her red-quartz steps along the River Neva,

when I thought of her near the Old Bourse, I fell down
and I wept—

I could see God for a second as traces of yellow sun
moved across her body in the casket the old Italian men
laid her out in,

her voice speaking in tongues inside my head as though
she was a colporteur now getting to live that grand life
along the old blood roads of Octavio Paz,

her body smooth and cold as ice,
but I had to touch it all the same (just to be sure).

But now I know she is gone forever, and I am finally
ready to receive forgiveness for all my sins,

put the needle in my veins, and wait for the
spaceship to take me.

You Know Too Much About Flying Saucers

I dreamed a hole through her head, where blue
cathoray spilled out over space and time,

ten seconds of my stare, my eyes pretending to look
at the red Coca-Cola sign flashing up behind her head,
blinking on and off in reds and whites over and over:
Drink Coke—You Dope!

People say we are like Siamese twins, but really
we are more like Tiananmen Square, 1989;
six murdered sextuplets on a Sunday;

You're crazy. We can't be together, she says—this is
every time right before we go and remarry down in old
Mexico;

I love the crazy flashing skies over Acapulco, an
emerald stain the way George Stevens got to do it
on film,

both of us with bare feet, dancing under moonlight,
over broken bottles of glass, arms flailing, waving madly;

every day another séance to stop the Nuclear bombs,
all night long as we pray against the missiles landing
in someone else's backyard—

wet and on fire; a wave, ten thousand surfers going out
from the storm atop another tsunami; I can taste it! I can bury it
in the morning with my foot down to the floorboard;

water, napalm, flying about; I will fly; sea turtles flowing
in my veins to the other side of the earth; my mouth: it's
got a direct line to Jehovah's red ear, splitting my own
chest open to get down to that vodka with a straw;

swinging, dancing, spinning, tango atop the cobblestones,
both of us shivering along the gold spires, our souls being
pushed up hard against doors, in heavenly colors, azure-blue,
emerald, until we are falling one thousand years into the future—

down to the ghost of your words as they whisper out to me:
"divided together; and so we fall apart."

Arrete! C'est ici L'Empire de la Mort—

On that cold October day we escaped the Paris rain
by going down the spiral staircase of seventy-seven steps,
fifty feet below into the graffiti filled Catacombs of the
supernatural,

deeper and deeper we ran through the revolution of years,
black pools of underground rain collecting on the ceiling,
like years of rain that was supposed to quench and protect us,

you kept smiling, nervously laughing, your hand pulling at
your V-neck shirt, trying to cover over your breasts from the cold,
running and running through the years until we reached the painted
pillars, a doorway between them, where this sign stops you in your
tracks:

Stop! Here is the Empire of the Dead—

Into the room of the dead we rushed, russet and brown stained bones
piled atop each other as walls: arm and leg bones, ribs and shoulders,
men and women, the rich and the poor and the young and the old,

fast death /slow death,

the apple size eyes of their skulls staring out at us as we stood there
together, intricate patterns that are meticulously placed in both dignity
and symmetry, six million dead below the streets of Paris, France
(beating on anyway),

and you held my hand tight and leaned into me; and you whispered in my ear right then: "I wish I were dead sometimes, too!" you said;

and I knew what you meant, but I was afraid to admit it out of fear of egging you on.

John Updike

I tried to kill myself by reading
some poetry by John Updike.

—anonymous

I am running from the pain all the time now … you know the one,
that single empty chamber that has no name;

It runs in the dark door in extreme *pallor*,
a disgust quotient of 10 over 4 in our great American life—
that bomb coming through your doorway courtesy
of the USA;

a person disappearing, delicately *diaphanous* as they go
into the nothingness forever; shhhh! whispered; a kind of death
that we pretend God doesn't hear;

that bloody spot on the ground where someone once stood,

a spot where their child will stand twenty years from now,

—the *polychrome* buildings glimmering in the thin reflection
of God, his personal photog spinning around, over and over,
to get the picture.

Into The City

I asked her to take me to the city
where the suicides start at sundown,
each soul a fresh map in their latest crackup,
all the blue stars burning holes in the sky,

twilight the way Fitzgerald would have liked it—
Detroit as blue as a glacier; *I'll take what you got*
flashing up in red neon, over and over—

this girl likes to hold my hand,
her dreams are only slightly broken,
she knows all the stars' homes without
ever having to look at a map;

she looks in my blue eyes and says:
you could stop it if you wanted to;

I know it—I know;

in her bed she spreads her legs wide open,
she smells good like August, my fingers
taste like blueberries:
that wonderful scent within her deepest pain—
is that you and I in yesterday? are we drowning too?
try to swim to that island out there!

we wake up and it is night,
outside the seven fires are burning,

over there is where the grand canyon awaits us,
only it is metal and concrete, and it is really 3rd Street,

looking around my eyes are tired from all the wars,

that deepening sound of all the people I've let go of,
each one falling through the air like it is Sept. 11th all
over again,

and I'm falling now, too—falling like wet patina
in between the buildings,

my blood and soul red and black as it is tattooing the air

until it is too late.

The Things You Did When You Could Have Done Something Else

Ten so-called college poets slouch over a dictionary,
because they're all too cheap not to buy their own,

the rain brings a drowsiness, the mind traveling
downhill to a crocus lined brick path,

this is when he thinks of *her*:

her body shifting in sunlight as she showers
next to the rooftop sauna next door;

they are one—like farmers and loose earth,
their lips wet with wine and one another,
the blue sheets crumpling up from the grip
of their hands;

he wants to name his first three daughters after her,
he wants to tell her all of her jokes until she is red
in the face,

but right then he swerves off the path as the sun
begins to brighten outside on Highland Avenue,

M. exclaims: the three saddest words a man can say
to a woman!

R. answers: *There's someone else.*

Q. says: *I'm the boss.*

T. bursts out laughing: *The game's on.*

He looks over at the rest of them now, only seconds outside of his mind thinking of her and all that loose earth.

"I give up," he says to the other nine; all of them believing that he has totally missed the point yet again.

No. 5, 1948

We lit the candle directly at the center of the cul-de-sac,
recited all the right incantations to make your ghost reappear,

scared like naïve little children, we got so frightened that we
ran away into the tall timothy and alfalfa of the meadow next
to the abandoned golf course,

running all the way to the edge of the woods like white-tailed deer
run away,

and at the very top of the hill we suddenly could see two purple
sunsets, and they dripped out the sky like Jackson Pollock's
No. 5, 1948,

but the sun had already set that evening, and we all knew the
world was about to die, and that we were all going to die too—
that we had only a few seconds left.

Grand Canyon

You told me it took 40-million years to
form the Grand Canyon—the Vishnu Schist
2-billion years, the yellow-green light on the rim
of the Kaibab another 230-million;

but I know it only took a few days for everything
to fall apart: the morning hail of the white church
raining inside you all the way home,

the blue Colorado drifting you away on false notes,
tied up the way you asked to be, the war playing over
and over in your head until it was ready to explode,

the rock and sediment wearing us down,
all the rest of us spilling out from the inside,
until the core shows, beautiful in the platinum moonlight,
our bodies wet and wedged in between the glittering strata,
all the night stars shaking violently in the sky,

because we are leaving each other, like the night
is full of guilt, because that is when everyone
leaves each other: always under the cover of darkness.

Late Summer In Rhode Island

All of us natives hope for September again,
when the blueberries pop from their branches,
and the songbirds give us their last symphonies,

when we would trade it all in for one smiling face,
each one of us still in the warmth of our summer dreams—
that late time of the year when we miss each other the
most.

After ten days of storms over Rhode Island,
the red starfish litter the beach like it is the sky,
pools form in the middle of the golden dunes,
the black form of fishermen sway again down
in the salt ponds near Galilee,

and over on the Newport Bridge, the cars go sliding
forth like they will never be coming back again—*shhhh!*

Gun, With Occasional Music

Across the ocean nobody is dying,
but back here in the red, white, and blue of America
we are all still getting shot.

In the stress of our own disregard we begin
to say: *let's get rid of all of the guns*;

but it's hard to say this to a bunch of angry,
white men armed to the hilt with a stockpile
of automatic weapons.

And so, we all choose to ignore it and instead go
on out to all our favorite little Italian restaurants,

and you wear your beautiful silver dress,
and I wear the black Armani suit you bought
me for our anniversary;

we drink Mojito cocktails, and listen to haunting music
floating on the air out of WaterPlace Park,

fireworks soon shoot on up into the dark night
over Providence—

yellow weeping willow, orange spider web,

all of America still dying as these magical little jewels
dance and spin and light up before quickly fading back
to black.

Mohegan Bluffs

The ghosts sail out from the Charlestown
Breachway every night at dusk,

the wind filling their sails, shadow filled,
all these tiny pewter disks shining atop the
waves,

and sometimes you can hear them saying:
I just want to go home;

and they sail out into the Great Salt Pond
into the middle of Block Island, where the
parking is always free;

where all our familiar dreams go on vacation;
and when you're ready maybe you'll go there
too;

out into the mystery of happiness—
you and God in a perfect place,

out into a little secret that lasts no longer
than a second:

never desire anything.

Color-fields

Her house on White Street, still unpainted—
that Key West gray.

At Sloppy Joe's,
Jesus sits at the bar with Hemingway,

"There is no heaven," he whispers over to me.

The Hours Happened (9/11)

We drove out of Vendian and out into Ordovician,
The air moist and warm blowing through our hair,
New York City rising in gray vaults off on the horizon,
Abandoned dreams behind us in our rear-view mirror,

We stepped all through the hot ash after reaching ground zero,
Leaving only our footprints to prove that we were there,
A part of me couldn't grasp what had just happened,
You looked at me and said: "Can you describe all of this?"
I looked over at you and I said: "I don't think I ever can."

Young Brother

They all want to make him
a hero for his deadly disease,

but it is I who swam with him,
gave the gift of him,

the glint of bodies, naked,
down by the old Scituate reservoir,

growing up together,
not our religion, not our color,
not in the field where we were born,
not even our experiences together,

only the ghost of his life that begins
to waver in my arms; and him as he
begins to whisper in my ear:

I've been waiting for you.
I've been waiting for you.
I've been waiting so long
for you young brother!

Violent Acts of Beauty

In 1969, the world was born up in the Berkshires,
even though all the hotels were closing and mankind
was trying to escape out to the moon;

outside my bedroom window the entire street was
frozen in ice,

from Scituate all the way up to the glowing red stop sign
that sat at the edge of another life:

mothers serving cake and chocolate ice cream—*we don't want
the kids to know that they are dying!*

hints of it all, portraits carved out of stone on the faces
of people going by; but you don't want to look, so we
can all keep on pretending;

strange lives on the interior, wafting caverns inside
all of our emptiness,

souls painted a way that would befit our favorite
artist if he were to portray us within that darkness
of our very souls:

all desires suppressed, all thoughts pushed aside,
everything is perfect—

God everywhere and nowhere, a boat pushed gently
off away from the dock,

fleeting and exotic, billowing cloud and sky atop
the surface of the water as we all drift downstream—

six trips to Paris, two down to New Orleans;
fifty-seven to Key West, so you can get an idea
of who you really are this time;

toes touching the waves, ninety-seven chrome tumblers,
and you?—someone hidden behind the Venetian
colonnades in St. Mark's Square like a fool;

all humans like shafts of light falling on an empty
forest floor,

blue and abstract, like gulf waters, jealousy in
a freeze frame for a split second,

coming away from the blue sheets that we pull
down on our most supplicant guests: interiors
turned inside out all the way through the summer
months;

Pierre! I think his name was: that period that goes
at the very end of your life;

the wind wafting at the red and white striped
awnings …until there isn't a sound.

www.ingramcontent.com/pod-product-compliance
Lightning Source LLC
LaVergne TN
LVHW040028190726
843490LV00013B/992